Newcastle

Mike Wilson

Published in association with The Basic Skills Agency

Hodder & Stoughton

A MEMBER OF THE HODDER HEADLINE GROUP

Acknowledgements

Photos: pp. 2, 12, 22, 27, 32, 36 and 42 © Allsport,
        p. 8 © Hulton Getty.
Cover photo: © Allsport.

Orders: please contact Bookpoint Ltd, 39 Milton Park, Abingdon, Oxon OX14 4TD. Telephone: (44)
01235 400414, Fax: (44) 01235 400454. Lines are open from 9.00–6.00, Monday to Saturday, with a
24 hour message answering service. Email address: orders@bookpoint.co.uk

British Library Cataloguing in Publication Data
A catalogue record for this title is available from The British Library

ISBN 0 340 71169 8

First published 1998
Impression number 10 9 8 7 6 5 4 3
Year 2003 2002 2001 2000 1999

Typeset by Fakenham Photosetting Ltd, Fakenham, Norfolk,
Printed in Great Britain for Hodder & Stoughton Educational, a division of Hodder Headline Plc,
338 Euston Road, London NW1 3BH, by Redwood Books, Trowbridge, Wiltshire.

Contents

1 The Toon Army

It was March 1997.
An all-time low
for the Toon Army.

For two years we had hoped
to win the Premier League.
But our hopes had been dashed.

Kevin Keegan
(more a god than a man)
had left the club.

And now we were out
of the EUFA Cup.
We crashed out 4–0
against AS Monaco.

It can't get any worse!

St James' Park.

The Chairman of Newcastle
was Sir John Hall.
He spoke out for all the fans.
He said, 'Our pride is hurt.'

Newcastle's fans are called the 'Toon Army'.
The Toon Army is all about pride.
Football is not just a way of life.
Not in the North East.
It is life itself.
It is the heart and soul
of the Geordie Nation.

When the Toon Army support their team,
it is like having an extra player
on the pitch.

Win or lose,
home or away,
rain or shine:

We are proud to follow Newcastle United!

2 History

At first there were two teams.
They were Newcastle West End
and Newcastle East End.
The teams united on 9 December 1892.
Newcastle United had begun.

For the first two years,
United wore a red and white strip.
Red shirts and white shorts.
(Just like Middlesbrough today!)

The famous black and white stripes
came in 1894.

It was the black and white strip
that gave the team its nickname.
We are called 'the Magpies'.

United have had a long,
successful history.

We've won the League four times,
and the FA Cup six times.
We have also been in five other
FA Cup finals,
but lost each time.

We won the Fairs Cup in 1969,
and the FA Youth Cup in 1962 and 1985.

Our biggest win was 13–0
against Newport County in 1946.

Our worst ever home defeat was 9–1.
The good news is:
it was a long time ago – 1908.
The bad news is:
it was against a local side – Sunderland!

3 Hall of Fame

There have been many great players
at St James' Park over the years.

Jackie Milburn was a United player.

He played for us
for over ten years: 1946–1957.
He scored 200 goals
in nearly 400 matches.
He helped us win two FA Cup finals.

He died in 1988.
But his name lives on.
The Milburn Stand at St James' Park
is named after him.

Malcolm MacDonald
was known as SuperMac.
He was the most amazing
goal-scoring machine.

He played for Newcastle
from 1969 to 1976.

He scored a hat-trick
in his first match for the Magpies.

He scored five goals in
one match for England.
(But then it was against Cyprus!)

He scored after only five seconds
in a match in 1975.
It was a friendly against
St. Johnstone.

That's a record.
It will take some beating!

SuperMac!

Arthur Cox
was the Magpies' manager
from 1980 to 1984.
He brought some world-class players
to Tyneside:

Kevin Keegan,
Terry McDermott
and Peter Beardsley.

These three players
all played under Arthur Cox.
And they all came back
to St James' Park in the 1990s.
They just couldn't stay away!

In the meantime,
home-grown talent,
like Chris Waddle and Paul Gascoigne,
had made their names at Newcastle.

When Kevin Keegan came back to Tyneside
as United's manager,
he asked Arthur Cox to come back
and be his assistant.

4 Special K

United fans will never forget
the FA Cup Final of 1974.

The Magpies were facing
the great Liverpool side of the 1970s.
The Liverpool team had swept across Europe.
They had won everything in sight.

Newcastle lost 3–0 that day.
Not even SuperMac could save us!

And guess who scored two goals
and took the game out of our reach?

Kevin Keegan.

The man they called God
on Tyneside.
They also called him King Kevin.
Sometimes 'Special K'!

In years to come,
Keegan would come to the North East.
He would save Newcastle United.
Twice.

In 1982,
things were in a bad way
for Newcastle United.
We were drifting
very near the bottom of Division Two.

We could not think about playing
in Division Three.
We needed someone to inspire us.
Someone to save us
from a fate worse than death.

Kevin Keegan had played for Liverpool.
He had played for SV Hamburg in Germany.
For two years,
he was European Footballer of the Year.
In 1982 he got an OBE.

King Kevin.

That year,
Keegan came to Newcastle as captain.
He scored three goals in his first three games.
By the end of the season,
we were pushing for promotion!

In fact, Newcastle were promoted
the next season, 1983–84.
Keegan scored in the last match of the season.
(It was his 500th League match.)

Then Keegan retired.
He was 33 years old.
He wanted to spend his time
playing golf in Spain.

5 Keegan the Manager

Early in 1992.
It was the same old story again.

Newcastle were back in trouble,
back at the bottom of Division Two.
We were losing to teams
like Southend, Oxford
and Charlton.

Keegan took on the job
of saving Newcastle United
a second time.

And he did it – just.

It was the very last game of the season.
We needed to beat Leicester
to stay up.

In extra time,
Leicester scored an own goal.
Newcastle won 2–1,
and stayed in Division Two.

Next season we played Leicester again.
It was the very last game.
We had to win.
We wanted to go up.
We wanted to be in
the Premier League.

This time, we won 7–1!

Two new Newcastle players
got hat-tricks that day:
Andy Cole and David Kelly.

From the start,
Keegan had a master plan.
He wanted Newcastle to get to the top.
He wanted the team to stay there.

The plan was to spend, spend, spend.

In his first six months,
he spent over £2 million.
And after that,
it was more every year.

In 1993, he spent over £5 million.
In 1994, he spent over £11 million.
In 1995, it was over £15 million.

And in 1996, it was over £26 million.
And that was on just three players:

Faustino Asprilla,
David Batty and Alan Shearer.

Alan Shearer was the England captain.
He came to Tyneside from Blackburn.
This was in July 1996.
The fee was £15 million.
This was a World Record fee.

Keegan bought many new players.
In five years he spent over
£60 million.

He made a joke about it:
'When I came to Newcastle,
Sir John Hall was very rich.
Now he is just rich!'

The fans joked about it too.
They said that Keegan had a plan.
His plan would help Newcastle
to win the League.
It was to buy up all the best players.
Then no other team could
beat Newcastle.

6 Andy Cole

Andy Cole came from Bristol City
in 1993.
He quickly won the hearts
of Geordie fans.
('Geordie' is the nickname for
a person from Newcastle.)

How did he win their hearts?
By scoring goals!
He scored 41 in one season.
It was a club record,
and it is still unbeaten.

Andy Cole was at his best.
It took a brave man to sell him.
But that's just what Kevin Keegan did.

The Geordie fans were angry.
They wanted to know why.
It took a brave man to tell them.
But that's what King Kevin did.

'If I'm wrong,' he said,
'there's a bullet with my name on.'
In other words,
he was saying – 'Trust me.
I'll take the flak.
I know what I'm doing.'

7 Alan Shearer

Geordie fans were happy
when Kevin Keegan bought top players
like Andy Cole,
Les Ferdinand, David Ginola
and Faustino Asprilla to Newcastle.

But they were over the moon
when they heard that Alan Shearer
was coming home to Tyneside.

If anyone could help Newcastle
to win the big prizes,
it was the England Captain.

And the price?
A mere £15 million!
Worth every penny!

Shearer came to Newcastle
in July 1996.

Alan Shearer.

He had always wanted
to play for United.
Ever since he was a boy,
he had supported them.
When he was 12 years old,
he had gone to St James' Park
to watch his hero – Kevin Keegan.

Alan Shearer used to play
for Southampton.
Just like Kevin Keegan.
He scored a hat-trick
in his first full game for them.

Then he went to Blackburn.
His manager there was Kenny Dalglish.
Shearer scored two goals
in his first match for them.

He went on to score 128 goals
in 170 matches for Blackburn.

When he moved to Newcastle,
manager Kevin Keegan said:
'This is a signing
for the people and fans of Newcastle.'

Shearer said:
'Geordies will know
how proud this makes me feel.'

Shearer missed some of the 1996–97 season
due to injury.
But there was worse to come.

It was at the start of the 1997–98 season,
There was a friendly against Chelsea.
Shearer broke his ankle.

He would miss the start of the season.
He would miss important World Cup
matches for England.
He would be out of action for months.

To make things worse,
Newcastle had just sold Les Ferdinand
to Spurs for £6 million.

(Les didn't want to leave Tyneside,
and Kevin didn't want to sell him.
But the Newcastle Board said
that they needed the money.)

Suddenly,
our top two strikers were both gone
in the same week!

8 Faustino Asprilla

With Shearer out of action,
and with Ferdinand and Ginola
both sold to Spurs,
Tino Asprilla became
Newcastle's number one striker.

Tino is from Colombia,
in South America.
His nickname is
'The Black Arrow'.

He came to Tyneside in February 1996.
He came from Parma in Italy.
He cost £7.5 million.

When he first flew in to Newcastle,
he wore a big fur coat.
And on the football field,
he wore gloves,
because he was always cold!

Faustino Asprilla.

In his first match
he came on as a substitute,
with only 20 minutes to go.
It was a local derby
against Middlesbrough.

He was such an amazing player.
The Middlesbrough players
did not know what he would do next.

The trouble was,
the Newcastle players didn't know
what he would do next either!

But Tino helped United to win the match.

In September 1997,
Newcastle played Barcelona
in the European Champions' League.
It was a night to remember,
and Tino's finest hour.

We won 3–2,
and Tino scored a hat-trick.

Tyneside had a new hero!

9 The End of King Kevin

It was August 1996.
The start of a new football season.
Newcastle played Manchester United
in the FA Charity Shield.

But Newcastle lost 4–0.

We had lost out to Man United before,
at the end of the 1995–96 season.
They had won the League,
and we were second.
Kevin Keegan gave a TV interview.
He lost his temper.

Newcastle had thrown away a 12-point lead
in the League.
Man United had overtaken us.
'I'd love us to beat them!' he shouted.
But we didn't.

And in the next season –
they were doing it to us again!
Later on we got our revenge.
We hammered them 5–0
in October 1996.
This was the worst defeat
Alex Ferguson had ever known!

But the new season
had not got off to a very good start.
And it wasn't just Man United.
We lost to Coventry and
Nottingham Forest.
We lost to Arsenal,
when they were down to ten men.

By January 1997, it was clear.
We weren't going to win anything that year.
Kevin Keegan packed his bags
and left Newcastle United.

It wasn't the first time
he had stormed out.
But it was definitely the last time.

Two days later,
Newcastle beat Spurs 7–1!
But not even that
made Keegan change his mind.

Kevin Keegan the manager.

His team had cost over £60 million.
They were the best
that money could buy.
His forwards were the envy of the world.
But the defence could always
let in goals.
We lost so many games
that we should have won!

In the end, Keegan saw
that his exciting style of football
was not enough.

You can win matches.
You can thrill the crowds.
But you can't always
win championships.

When Kevin Keegan left,
he took the world by surprise.
Yet again.

Waddington's
the people who make toys and games,
had to stop making football cards
with his picture on!

But, once he had gone,
King Kevin didn't sit around
with nothing to do.
He had plans to write his life story.
He had plans to write a book about football.

And he had plans
to put a football game show on TV.

But it wasn't long before he was
managing a football team again.
In September 1997,
the millionaire, Mohammed Al Fayed,
asked him to take over at Fulham.

Some said that Kevin was back again,
doing what he did best –
spending a millionaire's money!

10 King Kenny?

Kenny Dalglish
took over Newcastle United
a week after Kevin Keegan resigned.

He knew already
there were some big problems at the club.
He knew he had some re-building to do.
He knew it would take time.

Kevin Keegan had said:
'If the Newcastle Board of Directors
ever say "no"
when I want to sign a new player,
then I'll know my time is over.'

But Kenny Dalglish had no plans
to spend his way out of trouble.
His style is different.

Kenny Dalglish.

When he came to Tyneside,
Kenny Dalglish knew
that he had some world class stars.
But he also knew
that team work is more important
than any one man's talent.

Kenny Dalglish planned to
build us a dream team.
Just like he did at Liverpool
and Blackburn Rovers.

But at the very start
of the 1997 season,
Kenny's dream team was hit by injury.

Shearer was out.
Batty was injured for a while.
So was Asprilla,
and new signing, Stuart Pearce.

Dalglish was desperate.
He signed John Barnes from Liverpool,
and Ian Rush from Leeds.
Even though they were both over 30.

One writer said that
Dalglish was setting up a rest home
for all his old Liverpool mates!

But Kenny showed
he could buy young blood too
– with Tomasson, Pistone and Ketsbaia
all coming from abroad.

The slow re-building had begun.
But it was all too slow for Kenny Dalglish.

In August 1998,
Dalglish was sacked.

Newcastle's first match of the 98–99 season
was against Charlton Athletic.
They were new in the Premier League.
Everyone knew they'd go straight back down
to Division One.
Charlton were down to ten men,
but all the Magpies could manage was a 0–0 draw.

Dalglish had led the Toon Army to Wembley,
to the FA Cup Final that year.
But they lost 2–0 to Arsenal.

Still no glory for the Magpies!

Ruud Gullit got Dalglish's job.

Dalglish was bitter:
'Maybe Ruud would like my new house as well!'
he said angrily.

Ruud got a hero's welcome on Tyneside.
He promised to bring 'sexy football' with him.

But he knew there was a lot of hard work to do.

He knew he'd have to win something
to keep the Toon Army on his side.

Ruud's contract runs out in June 2001.
Do you think he will stay until then?

In the same year,
Alan Shearer's playing contract runs out.
Shearer will be in his early 30s by then.
He may be looking for a change.
He may be looking for a new job in football . . .

Who do you think United's next manager will be?

The Newcastle squad.